# YOUR KNOWLEDGE HAS VALUE

- We will publish your bachelor's and
  master's thesis, essays and papers

- Your own eBook and book -
  sold worldwide in all relevant shops

- Earn money with each sale

Upload your text at www.GRIN.com
and publish for free

Marcio Hemerique Pereira

# The Modern Eye: Literature and the Art Aesthetics - "The Moon and Sixpence"

GRIN Verlag

**Bibliografische Information der Deutschen Nationalbibliothek:**

Die Deutsche Bibliothek verzeichnet diese Publikation in der Deutschen National-
bibliografie; detaillierte bibliografische Daten sind im Internet über http://dnb.d-
nb.de/ abrufbar.



**Imprint:**

Copyright © 2011 GRIN Verlag GmbH
Druck und Bindung: Books on Demand GmbH, Norderstedt Germany
ISBN: 978-3-656-35014-9

**This book at GRIN:**

# THE MODERN EYE: LITERATURE AND THE ART AESTHETICS-
## *'THE MOON AND SIXPENCE'*

Marcio Hemerique Pereira

Birkbeck College

University of London

"Why should you think that beauty, which is the most precious thing in the world, lies like a stone on the beach for the careless passer-by to pick up idly? Beauty is something wonderful and strange that the artist fashions out of the chaos of the world in the torment of his soul. And when he has made it, it is not given to all to know it. To recognize it you must repeat the adventure of the artist. It is a melody that he sings to you, and to hear it again in your own heart you want knowledge and sensitiveness and imagination [...]" (*The Moon and Sixpence*, Chapter XIX, p.153)

Only few contemporary authors have been praised as highly and condemned as completely as W. Somerset Maugham. The present essay discusses Maugham's novel *'The Moon and Sixpence.'*[1] My concerns lay on key questions that I try to explore. First and foremost, what do we learn about the presentation of the early twentieth century artist from Maugham? Are, in fact, artistic techniques used in the literary portrait (depictions) of the artist? What do we learn about modern art from the text? Why is Maugham writing about an artist? How can literature depict artist and artistic processes? Now I propose to attempt at least to suggest the reasons for, if not to reconcile, opinions as widely different as the ones presented further in the essay and, at the same time, to offer a less impetuous and more carefully substantiated criticism of Maugham's fictional work, *'The Moon and Sixpence.'*

*'The Moon and Sixpence'* by William Somerset Maugham is a book that stands exceptional for its great presentation. It is said that the book is based on the life of the painter Paul Gauguin. The story is presented in first person narrative. In the story, Paul Gauguin appears as the fictional character Charles Strickland. It takes the reader to read the entire story to get a complete picture of the character as

---

[1] W. Somerset Maugham. *The Moon and Sixpence* (1919; New York: Penguin, 1977).

Maugham unfolds the character little by little in a gradual progression. To illustrate my point, in the beginning of the story, one can see a character that is presented as a super ordinary man. Maugham says "he was null. He was probably a worthy member of society, a good husband and father, an honest broker, but there was no reason to waste one's time over him" (Maugham, 24). Thus, with his mastery in using language, Maugham makes the reader believe that Strickland is an ordinary man.[2] One can see elaborate effort from the part of the writer to show the ordinary way of life led by Strickland and his wife. It is said "they would see their son and daughter come to years of reason, marry in due course, the one a pretty girl, future mother of healthy children, the other a handsome manly fellow, obviously a soldier, and at last, prosperous in their dignified retirement, beloved by their descendents, after a happy, not unuseful life."[3] (Maugham, 26)

However, things change dramatically thereafter. One day, he just moves to Paris leaving his family behind. It was the writer who was appointed to meet Strickland in Paris and to bring him back. However, when the writer asks "Then, what in God's name have you left her for?" Strickland simply says that "I want to paint" (Maugham, 49). Thus, one can see an effort from the part of Maugham to express the idea that the call of art is much stronger than all other temptations, or that the artist is beyond all social influences. At this stage, Strickland appears totally emotionless and indifferent. As the writer admits, "I could not struggle against his indifference". (Maugham, 42) However, at this particular point, the presentation of the character Strickland has only reached the half way. Much more is there to come. Dirk Stroeve and his wife appear from nowhere to help Strickland, and then to fall prey to his unpredictable and paradoxical nature. Strickland, who said he had no emotional attachment to his pretty wife or family, falls in love with Stroeve's wife. When the writer says "I never knew a man so entirely indifferent to his surroundings", (Maugham, 82) the indifferent man had the other man's wife in his mind, thus taking a 'U' turn. However, soon she commits suicide, possibility at the end of the infatuation she felt for the better, as females are destined to do. Then there is Ata,

---

[2] In 'The Moon and Sixpence.' Charles Strickland leaves his wife and his position as a stockbroker to go to Paris to paint. Still stifled, he leaves for Tahiti, where he finds Paradise, a beautiful natural country, and Eve in the person of Ata, a woman who will care for him and ask nothing in return. He is free to create. Strickland is also free from public opinion and criticism. He says many times that he is not interested in the opinions of others; he wants only to paint.

[3] For comments on this point, see M.K. Naik, *W. Somerset Maugham* (Norman: University of Oklahoma Press, 1966), p.59-68; Robert Calder, *W. Somerset Maugham and the Quest for Freedom.* (London: Heinemann, 1972), p.138-158

another woman who stands by Strickland till the end. The story presents a Dorian Grey touch (from the great novel *The Picture of Dorian Grey* by Oscar Wilde) ending showing the marks of leprosy as the indication of the deterioration of his soul. Just like the beautiful Dorian who leads to the suicide of many admires before his destruction of himself and his portrait, Strickland ruins the life of many before he dies along with his masterpiece.

*

The story presents Maugham as a plain and straightforward writer who narrates stories according to the realms of Modernism.[4] The story transforms Gauguin into the fictional Charles Strickland, who abandons his wife and children and goes into a career 'to paint'.

In addition, one can see Maugham stressing on the daunting use of colour and stunning primitivism evident in the art of Strickland. It is said:

> "[...] the colours were so strange that words can hardly tell what a troubling emotion they gave. They were sombre blues, opaque like a delicately carved bowl in lapis lazuli, and yet with a quivering lustre that suggested the palpitation of mysterious life; they were purples, horrible like raw and putrid flesh, and yet with a glowing, sensual passion that called up vague memory of the Rome Empire of Heliogabalus; there were reds, shrill like the berries of holly- one thought of Christmas in England, the snow [...], [...] who can tell what anguished fancy made these fruits? [...]" (Maugham, 231-4)

One can say that this is the best possible narrative of a modern work in modern literature. Unlike other works that deals with a rather complicated life and ends by unfolding the mystery surrounding it, Maugham starts from the simplicity of Strickland's life and ends in total confusion facing the complexity of his nature and his work. Thus, one can see an effort from this modernist writer to show that modern art is difficult to interpret, and modern artist is beyond the realm of society.

---

[4] Rosemary Sumner. *A Route to Modernism,* Basingstoke: Palgrave Macmillan, 2000

Jones pointed out in his intriguing essay *'W. Somerset Maugham: An Appreciation'* that Maugham's technique is "a technique that almost deliberately limits his emotional range", that is because "his picture of the artist in *'The Moon and Sixpence'*, and that of the novelist in *'Cakes and Ale'*, are pictures of particular artists in particular situations, not of the artist in general; in his presentation of them we miss that final probing insight which reveals the universal through the particular." [5]

However, it seems that Maugham owes a lot to Conrad for this first-person narrative which collects information about the subject quite later, especially after his death. In addition, the temporal complexities and the fore-grounded story telling style resemble the Conrad of *'Heart of Darkness'* (1899). In the novel, the writer is a protagonist named 'Marlow' who took a foreign assignment from a Belgian trading company as a ferry-boat captain in Africa. His more important assignment was to return Kurtz, another ivory trader, back to civilization from Africa. In the novel too, Kurtz, the mysterious character dies, and later on, the writer pays a visit to the woman Kurtz was engaged to marry. The woman still thinks Kurtz was a noble man, and the writer even lies that his last word was her name. Now, in *'The Moon and Sixpence'*, one can see the writer paying a visit to Strickland's family and still hiding the facts about Ata and her children.

However, other people like Joyce, Woolf, and D. H. Lawrence too adopted the same method of seeking meaning in visionary figures, and all had irony as a main content. However, Maugham approaches the visionary figure with a lot of suspicion, and at every juncture, Maugham finds it difficult to find any meaning in the action of his visionary figure.

At first, one will feel that that Maugham is in dispute with the aestheticism. However, a closer look at his work proves that he is not against aestheticism at all. Instead, he simply tries to unveil the hollowness of the aesthetic belief in the privilege of beauty. It seems that both Maugham and his character Strickland are the supporters of aestheticism that advocates the separation of morality from artistic value. There were a number of artists who supported this late 19th century and early 20th century movement. Some of them were Charles Baudelaire, Aubrey Beardsley, Max Beerbohm, Gustave Flaubert, J. K. Huysmans, Stephane Mallarme, Walter

---

[5] Klaus W. Jonas. *W. Somerset Maugham: An Appreciation.* Books Abroad, Board of regents of the University of Oklahoma. Vol.33, No. 1 (Winter, 1959), pp.20-23

Pater, James McNeill Whistler, and Oscar Wilde, as well as Virginia Woolf herself. However, Maugham does not answer the question as to what are the motives that force an artist to create works of art in the face of untold difficulties.

**

The novel speaks volumes about the presentation of Gauguin.[6] In the novel, one can see two descriptions about the paintings of Strickland. One is on the walls of the hut in Tahiti, where Strickland met the end of his life.[7] About that picture, Maugham says that it was indescribably wonderful and mysterious. It filled him with an emotion which he could not understand or analyze. He felt the awe and delight which a man might feel who watched the beginning of the world. It was tremendous, sensual, and passionate; and yet there was something horrible there. It was the work of a man who delved into the hidden depths of nature and discovered secrets which were beautiful and fearful (Maugham, 226). This statement from Maugham seems an effort to remind the readers that the complexities of art beyond the knowledge of common wisdom is to be respected and revered, thus showing an admirable contemplation of modern art.

At this connection, one should check how Maugham describes another piece of work by Strickland. The picture was a fruit-piece; a pile of oranges, bananas, and mangoes. However, the writer points out that the colours were so strange that words could not explain the emotions they created. About the sombre blue, the writer says that it is opaque like a delicately carved bowl in *lapis lazuli* and yet with a quivering lustre that suggested palpitation of mysterious life. And about purple, the writer says

---

[6] *'The Moon and sixpence'* (1919) was Maugham first popular success, although ironically it lacks nearly all the elements considered necessary in popular fiction. Most of its early readers knew nothing of Gauguin, whose fantastic career suggested the story. Here is the classic portrayal of the genius who sacrifices everything – comfort, security, family, honour, health – to his art. Nothing else matters. However, the reader forms a measure of admiration for Strickland, who places above everything else the necessity for living his own life in his own way, and he succeeds. To him life is not a failure. It places then, the novel in an unforgettable place. Although it is almost self-evident that the novel is "about" Gauguin, to the point that the novel has contributed substantially to the Gauguin legend, this new starting point in Maugham's fiction is actually "about" the writer himself, and about the demands and effects of creation on the personality of the artist.

[7] As Liebman points out "to most critics, the central figure in Somerset Maugham's novel is Charles Strickland. The narrator's putative purpose is to examine Strickland's life and work in order to determine his real nature. The primary function of the other characters in the novel is to throw some light on the painter's personality, and these partial illuminations help the narrator in his attempt to explain Strickland's motivation.' (p.329) In Sheldon W. Liebman, *Fiction as Fantasy: The Unreliable Narrator in The Moon and Sixpence*. English Literature in Transition, 1880-1920, Volume 38, Number 3, 1995, pp.329-343. Published by ELT Press

that it is like raw and putrid flesh but having a flow with sensual passion that brought the memories of the Roman Empire of Heliogabalus, as previously mentioned. In addition, there were deep yellows that died with unnatural passion into a green as pure as the sparkling water of a mountain brook. The writer (p.231) admits that no one can tell what 'anguished fancy' made Strickland create that painting. One can undoubtedly say that Maugham has expressed great literary wizardry in depicting the pictures made by Strickland, or Maugham possessed very clear idea about the work by Gauguin or Post-Impressionism. According to Bassett, Maugham has come to represent everything that Modernists resisted and Epstein concludes:

> "His writing was an affront of them. He was apolitical and he wrote dead against the grain of modernism, with all its difficulty, preferring instead to write as plainly as possible about complex things. Maugham also had popular and financial success that most Modernists did not enjoy, and which, whether true or not, give the impression of a compromised artistic integrity." (134) [8]

In fact 'The moon and sixpence' helped unfold the Gauguin mythology in which a wilful man relinquishes his material comforts and goes to the South Sea in pursuit of the surroundings that enhance his art. In fact, the natural warmth of the South Seas is vividly expressed in his art. [9]

In 'The moon and Sixpence' Gauguin becomes a fictional character - Charles Strickland- who abandons his wife, children and his profession as a stockbroker and leaves for Paris as he wants to paint. From there, he moves to Marseilles and from there to Tahiti where he meets his end. Seeing the narrative and structure of 'The Moon and Sixpence', one can say that the modern story with

---

[8] Joseph Epstein, "Is It All Right to Read Somerset Maugham?" New Criterion 4.3 (1985), p.10. In: W. *Somerset Maugham: An Annotated Bibliography of Criticism, 1969-1997* by Troy James Bassett. English literature in Transition, 1880-1920, Volume 41, Number 2, 1998, pp.133-184. Published by ELT Press

[9] It reminds us that the novel was based on the life and legend of Paul Gauguin (1848-1903), the postimpressionist French painter who crucially influenced modern art with his shocking primitivism and daunting use of colour. The tropics, had long symbolized a freedom of imaginative expressiveness in the history of Romantic aesthetics, and Gauguin came to represent this symbolism perhaps more clearly than any other single modern artist. See Isidoro Montiel, "Gauguin in Literature and Art." Hobbies Feb 1972: 68-69. It gives a brief biography of Gauguin and lists *The Moon and Sixpence* as one of a few works that feature Gauguin. Notes the numerous departures from Gauguin's life that Maugham makes since "overall, the human puzzle of Gauguin [...] interested Maugham" more than accuracy.

flashbacks and discontinuity is very similar to Conrad's Heart of Darkness. In that novel, Charlie Marlow, the narrator, chases the visionary Kurtz into Congo. Such other works that depict artist stories are '*A Portrait of the Artist as a Young Man*' (1916) by James Joyce, and '*Death in Venice*' (1912) by Thomas Mann. In both these cases, one can see a glorification of the pain and suffering of the artist.

However, one can see the influence of two contradictory feelings in '*The Moon and Sixpence*'. On the one hand, Maugham too is aware like Woolf about the dangers of self-indulgence.[10] The realist in him bridles at the possibilities of a poetic language that can be brought about by self-indulgence and inwardness. However, Maugham seem embracing the same first person narrative method to get on with his story.

It is seen that if Victorian novelists wrote fiction as an indirect way to re-enter the social world from which they had been excluded or which they were afraid to enter directly, for the modernists, it was the way to identify themselves outside the norms of the social world and to conform their special status as artists. They did not like to live in these societies but wanted to go to the land of their creations where life was more honest and true to the feelings of their hearts. It helped them to look at the society from a different angle and criticize it when necessary. This separateness can be seen in Woolf, Joyce, and Lawrence where the individual's life is seen separate from the society. Moreover, in these modern fictions, like '*Ulysses*' and '*Women in Love*', the narrator and the protagonists are both separate from the community that is morally corrupt. However, Woolf too was struggling with the problem of how to extract the troublesome ego from the narrative voice. In her diary entry for Monday, January 20 she writes "I suppose the danger lies in the damned egotistical self; which ruins Joyce and [Dorothy] Richardson, to my mind. Is one pliant and rich enough to provide a wall for the book from oneself without its becoming, as in J&R, narrowing and restricting? Anyhow, there's no doubt the way lies somewhere in that direction; I must grope and still experiment [. . .]" (13-14)[11]

A closer look at Maugham's work will reveal the fact that this evident chaos in his creation is the result of two contradicting influences. The first one is the social

---

[10] The questions of narrative with which I am concerned here come together suggestively in Gillian Beer's "*Beyond Determinism: George Eliot and Virginia Woolf*," in her '*Arguing with the Past*.' London, 1989, pp.117-37.

[11] Cited in Joseph Allen Boone. *Libidinal Currents: Sexuality and the Shaping of Modernism*. US: University of Chicago Press, 1998. p.175

realism of the late Victorian period. This social realism is more evident in '*Liza of Lambeth*' (Maugham). An equal power is exerted by the Romantic aestheticism or impressionism. While reading the suicide of Blanche Stroeve in '*The Moon and Sixpence*,' one remembers the Sybil Vane in '*Picture of Dorian Gray*' (1891) by Oscar Wilde. In both the cases, one can see the death of heroine who symbolizes realism as a protest against the misdeeds of, or waywardness of aesthetic antiheroes. In addition, aestheticism is presented as something that is beyond the common norms of society and something that is to be dreaded. In other words, according to Maugham, Strickland forgot to see the sixpence (that is commonplace wisdom) when he went to capture the moon (that is aesthetic impulse). One can see a long list of writers ranging from Conrad, Joyce, Woolf, and D. H. Lawrence who looked for meaning in visionary figures.

One can say that writers like Raymond Chandler, Ian Fleming, and John Le Carre seemed following the Maugham style of heroes full of swagger and sweat, believing in the hollowness of aestheticism. In total, it becomes evident that the Moon and sixpence is a combination of the Victorian Realism and Modernism. The beauty of the work is its suspense and uncertainty regarding the moral implications of aestheticism and realism.

***

The French symbolism which began during 1880s has its influence on the work of Maugham too. In fact, as Habib (17) comments, French symbolic aesthetics rejected the ideology that art is meant to represent the world in the way it appears; in addition, it was proposed that art should be suggestive.[12] This should offer the reader, viewer, or listener the experience of truth, beauty or idea beyond mortal reality. Thus, a look into '*The Moon and Sixpence*' will reveal the fact that Maugham was an expert in this field. The reality that Maugham wanted to unveil in his novel was the meaninglessness of life and the nearly uncontrollable impulse of artistic creation.

---

[12] M. A. R Habib. *Modern Literary Criticism and Theory: A History*. New Delhi: Blackwell Publishing, 2008.

One can see that Maugham possesses a very clear idea about the post-impressionist painting. The post-impressionism was an effort to bring some order to the impressionism. So, objects were reduced to their basic shapes and vibrant colours were used. Van Gogh, Gauguin and Matisse are all considered the pioneers in post-impressionism. However, as Gantefuhrer-Trier (7), one cannot turn a blind eye towards the influence of cubism presented in 'The Moon and Sixpence;' and Cubism had its beginning in the beginning of 1900s from Pablo Picasso.[13] In Cubist artistic works, the subjects are depicted from various points of view to create a greater context. In such works, a shallow ambiguous space is created by interpenetrating surfaces at random angles. Maugham says, 'In addition, there were deep yellows that died with unnatural passion into a green as pure as the sparkling water of a mountain brook.' (Maugham, 231).

The reason as to why Maugham resorted to depicting the life of Gauguin is a matter that still remains mysterious. His works were enormously sumptuous with vibrant colours. In fact, Gauguin's self portrait reveals that he himself portrayed in various ways from Christ to Demon. It can be this paradoxical nature that inspired Maugham who wanted to narrate the friction between social realism and aestheticism. Maugham could find no better character than Gauguin in complexities and lawlessness. He abandons his family at a very later age, he who left a beautiful wife steals another man's wife, who helped him, and results in her suicide. Even without the slightest hint of remorse, he leaves for Africa where he lives with another woman, and he seems not at all deterred or influenced by the social norms. He is only concerned about painting. Thus, it becomes evident that the life of Gauguin, which originally was more complicated than the story, easily attracted Maugham.

However, the main purpose of the work seems to be that Maugham wanted to convey to his readers the forces behind aesthetic creation. The uncontrollable urge shown by Strickland in the novel is nodded approval by the literati. It is pointed out in 'Torossian' (145) that artists create not primarily for pleasure, but for the inner satisfaction.[14] It can be compared to eating to satisfy appease, though in both the cases, pleasure is a by-product. A look into history will prove that there were many artists who faced tortures and privations in pursuit of art. Some examples are Millet,

---

[13] Anne Gantefuhrer-Trier. *Cubism.* Germany: Taschen, 2004.
[14] *A Guide to Aesthetics* by Aram Torossian. (California: Stanford University. Press); London: Oxford University Press, Humphrey Milford. 1937

Berlioz, and Cezanne. About Whistler, it is said that he used to faint due to the fatigue given by his work. About Cezanne, it is said that he used to forget his canvas in the fields as he used to see a flame rising before his soul.

Another point is that the artist, through his creativity, builds an imaginative world where he is able to see the realization of his unbounded aspirations and desires. In addition, as *'A Guide to Aesthetics'* (Torossian, 148) puts it, the hero of an artist always contains a piece of the artist's soul; thus, the art work exhibits the artist's self, or a tendency the artist's conscience wants to exhibit, though with guilt. Thus, it becomes evident that if Maugham shows attachment to neither social realism nor aestheticism, the reason is that Maugham himself possessed a soul that was as calamitous as that of Gauguin, and it was this similarity that made Maugham closely follows the life of Gauguin with such a great degree of precision. However, Maugham seems to possess two ends; one that finds the undeniable urge as that was found by Strickland, and the other that can identify the issues of common wisdom and social reality.

In total, it becomes evident that *'The Moon and Sixpence'* by Maugham is a great piece of work that unveils the contradiction or friction between social realism and aestheticism. In addition, it succeeds, to a great extent, in depicting the agonising life of an artist. Also, it succeeds in showing how the quest of an artist for artistic fulfilment is seen absurd and wayward by the society as the ideologies of art, especially aesthetic ideology, are in sharp contrast with the common wisdom of the society. In short, Maugham in *'The Moon and Sixpence'* takes a position that neither abhors aesthetic creativity nor disfavours the common wisdom of the society. It only reminds the readers of the inevitable friction.

# Works Cited


Bassett, Troy James. W. *Somerset Maugham: An Annotated Bibliography of Criticism, 1969-1997*. English literature in Transition, 1880-1920, Volume 41, Number 2, 1998, pp.133-184. Published by ELT Press

Beer, Gillian. "*Beyond Determinism: George Eliot and Virginia Woolf*," in 'Arguing with the Past.' London, 1989, pp.117-37

Boone, Joseph Allen. *Libidinal Currents: Sexuality and the Shaping of Modernism*. US: University of Chicago Press, 1998

Conrad, Joseph. *Heart of Darkness*. Plain Label Books, 1975

Epstein, Joseph. *"Is It All Right to Read Somerset Maugham?"* New Criterion 4.3 (1985)

Gantefuhrer-Trier, Anne. *Cubism*. Germany: Taschen, 2004

Habib, M. A. R. *Modern Literary Criticism and Theory: A History*. New Delhi: Blackwell Publishing, 2008

Jonas, Klaus W.. *W. Somerset Maugham: An Appreciation*. Books Abroad, Board of regents of the University of Oklahoma. Vol.33, No. 1 (Winter, 1959), pp.20-23

Liebman, Sheldon W.. *Fiction as Fantasy: The Unreliable Narrator in The Moon and Sixpence*. English Literature in Transition, 1880-1920, Volume 38, Number 3, 1995, pp.329-343. Published by ELT Press

Maugham, W. Somerset. *The Moon and Sixpence* (1919; New York: Penguin, 1977)

Maugham, W. Somerset. *Liza of Lambeth*. USA: Serenity Publishers, 2008

Montiel, Isidoro. "Gauguin in Literature and Art." Hobbies, Feb 1972, pp.68-69.

Sumner, Rosemary. *A Route to Modernism,* Basingstoke: Palgrave Macmillan, 2000

Torossian, Aram. *A Guide to Aesthetics.* (California: Stanford University Press), London: Oxford University Press, Humphrey Milford, 1937

Wilde, Oscar. *The Picture of Dorian Gray: Easy Read Super Large 24pt*. US: Read How You Want, 2008